HOW TO DISAPPEAR

Amanda Dalton was born in 1957 in Coventry. After taking a degree in English and Art, she went to Durham University where she trained to be a teacher. She worked in Leicestershire comprehensive schools and as a Youth Theatre leader, and was a Deputy Headteacher for five years.

In 1994 she was awarded an East Midlands Arts Board writers' bursary and in 1995 she completed an MA in Writing at the University of Glamorgan. The same year she left teaching to become a Centre Director for the Arvon Foundation at Lumb Bank in West Yorkshire. In 1999 she took up her present job of Education Director at the Royal Exchange Theatre, Manchester.

She has published two pamphlets, *The Dad Baby* (Waldean Press, 1994) and *Room of Leaves* (Jackson's Arm, 1996), and has won prizes in several major poetry competitions. She has co-written and devised work for youth theatre and a dramatisation of *Room of Leaves* was broadcast on BBC Radio 4 in October 1998. She is currently completing a collaborative project, *The Desire Paths*, with photographer Claire McNamee.

AMANDA DALTON

Amanda Dalton.

HOW TO
DISAPPEAR

To Richard,

With very best wishes,

Amanda.

Lumb Bank
September '09

BLOODAXE BOOKS

ISBN: 1 85224 500 X

First published 1999 by
Bloodaxe Books Ltd,
P.O. Box 1SN,
Newcastle upon Tyne NE99 1SN.

Bloodaxe Books Ltd acknowledges
the financial assistance of Northern Arts.

Cover printing by J. Thomson Colour Printers Ltd, Glasgow.

Printed in Great Britain by
Cromwell Press Ltd, Trowbridge, Wiltshire.

Acknowledgements

Acknowledgements are due to the editors of the following publications in which some of these poems – or versions of them – first appeared: *BBC Wildlife Magazine, Blade, Bound Spiral, The Forsaken Merman* (Hodder & Stoughton, 1998), *Kunapipi, London Magazine, The North, Orbis, The Rialto, Smiths Knoll, Soundings, Staple* and *Writing Women*.

'Fisherman's Tale' was a prizewinner in the 1994 National Poetry Competition. 'Oil Scare' was a prizewinner in the 1995 BBC Wildlife Poetry Competition. 'Out of the Blue' was a prizewinner in the 1996 National Poetry Competition. 'How To Disappear' was a prizewinner in the 1997 Bridport Competition.

Some of these poems have appeared in two pamphlet collections, *The Dad Baby* (Waldean Press, 1994) and *Room of Leaves* (Jackson's Arm, 1996), and several have been broadcast on BBC Radio 4.

A dramatised version of *Room of Leaves* was broadcast on BBC Radio 4 in October 1998.

I am enormously grateful for the encouragement, honest criticism and support of many friends at the various stages of putting together this book. In particular, thanks to Barbara Bentley, Catherine Byron, Pamela Johnson, Sheenagh Pugh, Carole Satyamurti, Mahendra Solanki and Alicia Stubbersfield. Also to the Arvon Foundation at Lumb Bank, where it all started, and to David Groves, without whom...

Contents

I. BREATHING SPACES

The Dad-Baby

After your death, the fortune teller
told me to expect you
so I took to sitting in the dark
doing a kind of meditation.

Sometimes I thought I nearly saw you
gathering shape by the mantelpiece
and once I almost heard your voice
at the back of my neck –

but I was trying too hard,
so instead I watched TV
and started leaving all the lights on,
and sure enough that was when you came.

The trouble was you came as the Dad-Baby,
all hunched and cramped
in a pram that was never ours.
Only your grey eyes were familiar

and your gold tooth
grotesque in an infant's face.
Old balloon-head bobbing up
and back behind the blue canvas hood;
then you were gone.

Out of the Blue

She remembered gulls at night
were floating stars on the dark sea
and shattered windscreen was blossom
that fell silently, dissolving in your palm.

She remembered what an expert she had been
at lying in bed pretending to have died;
(the barbed-wire fear at the base of her spine,
the hardly breathing) and how easily metal crumples
if you hit it hard, just so.

Out of the blue, in her dream,
she would come round the edge of the quarry
at dusk. She would run up the muddied bank
to a path that led to the edge, to a drop for miles,
and a view, a panorama of the town and sea
and sand and the flat wide field
specked with bushes and pools,
and she could never tell if this was a place
she had seen or a place she would one day see
or if this was only a dream.

She remembered her grandad puppet
tangled up on the shelf –
his neck bent so far back,
wires so hopelessly crossed,
that she had taken scissors from the sewing box
and cut him free.

She remembered the flinch in her stomach,
the desperate regret, as she saw
how his limbs wouldn't dance, how he lolled,
how she would never be able to bear him like this.

Out of the blue she saw the flash
that exploded deep in her head
and she knew that the beach she had spilled onto
was motorway, and that gulls were headlights in her eyes,
and that she was lying far too close to the waves

that soaked her legs and almost deafened her
so that at first she didn't hear her grandad puppet moaning,
didn't feel the twist of guilt in the small of her back
like metal, cold and burning, as he fought for breath,
fought to find a way out of the shoebox
where she had buried him beneath the heavy soil.

And she couldn't remember the way to say she was sorry
and it was far too dark to find the path
that would take her back from the beach and the wide flat field
to the edge of the quarry and, in any case,
she suddenly realised, she was fighting for breath
and she couldn't move her legs, she couldn't move her legs at all.

On the Antrim Coast

By the time the helicopter came the whale had died,
the limb of a giant cast up on the churned sand.

All afternoon the kids had run to it
with their buckets full of sea, and we had tried to turn it,

pushing our weight at its impossible mass,
willing it to find its own way back.

We felt it die against our hands like something breaking
far away. The kids stopped in their tracks.
The helicopter turned in the grey air.

*

Sometimes a colour seeps into the water from the sky
or from the land. No one swam next day.

The sea was black. The skin of the whale had parched
and faded in the shifting tide. Other children traced its map

of barnacles and calluses and silk, while men with cameras
knelt in the sand to frame the thirty foot of it in a single shot.

We watched from the street as our kids carried their shoes
along the strandline, filling them with stones
to circle the whale, marking out its edge.

*

The boys drove onto the beach in a hail of sand
and long before they saw the knives the children knew.

They backed into the sea with their hands full of stones.
The boys ran at the whale.

Dark muscles of wave hit the shore as they stabbed
and stabbed until they severed the tail.

The children stared with ancient faces. A seagull yelled.
Then something deeper started echoing
for miles across the sand.

Oil Scare

For weeks you could write your name
in the grease on Henson's window,
follow a smear of boots up the track
to the croft – and the tea:
there was always something floating,
a film on the milk,
a whiff of kerosene,
that carried you to fields of darkened turnips,
sheep eating grass they shouldn't eat,
cows wedged into Mrs Burgess' yard.

And her youngest lad
down at the edge of the storm
where water explodes in your eyes,
watching the guillemots circle and dive
at the thick black tide.
They're committed to the sea,
he screamed across the wind.
The water's dying, and you thought
they were the strangest words
to hear from a boy.

Dog Running

And then it was a speck on the dunes,
barking in time to its run,
the same bark, she heard
as a shout of *Yes. Yes. Yes.*

She ran after it, yelling so loud
the wrong dogs appeared on the sand
and ran with her, licking her fingers,
brushing her legs with their thick, damp tails.

But it was gone, so she slowed to a walk,
stared at the sea and the silent hills,
knowing she'd come back in the dark

and walk the beach for hours,
like an idiot, shaking a box of biscuits,
banging a fork on a tin of meat,

without the first idea of how to think
like a dog or run with a scent,
ignoring the tracks
and the warnings of high tides.

One of the dogs dropped a pebble at her feet,
danced backwards, staring, stupid,
intent on a game. She tested the weight
of stone in her palm. Just once.

Snails

You cleared the ground and planted hostas.
We watched their leaves uncurl, some frilled and edged
with cream, some lemon-green, my favourites ridged
and tall and almost blue. But then, before
they had a chance to flower, the snails came.

At first only a nibbled edge of leaf
to show for it, a single hole, a tear,
until great ribbons shred, a mass of tiny
perforations like an acid spill.
One day entire leaves had disappeared.

For weeks I gathered snails into a bag,
carried them to next door's undergrowth
and tipped them free. But you were right –
when they returned they'd multiplied, their shells
were harder, some had learned to slide up trees.

That night you emptied bags of cooking salt
into a tub and whistled as you poured
the boiling water in. I followed paths
of glistening slime across the soil, took
the torch and shone it on your fingers as you
jabbed at shells, tugged and twisted snails
from leaves. We counted as they hit the water,
burning, drowning, shrivelling alive.

Next day their floating shells were beautiful,
like the domes of flooded palaces. I traced
the whorls and spirals etched in brown, the muted
blue and grey, the sunlit flash of green.
We never spoke again of killing snails.

Something has died in here,

something the cat dragged in and lost.
It's probably been festering for weeks
but hits us suddenly,
a stench that fills the freezing house
and makes me gag for air.

I dread the maggots most
but dream instead a vole falls down the chimney,
dead already. Its body twists and hisses
in the flame and skin around its teeth dissolves
until there's only bone and splitting fur
and smoke that stinks.

You move the sofa, shake out wellingtons,
shine a torch in every gap.
It's hopeless, there's no trail to follow.
Bring the dogs in, I say. *Watch the flies for clues.*
Give up. You light a fire, burn joss-sticks,
throw my perfume everywhere.

Making Space

For days the builders filled the house.
They lifted wood and fibre-glass
into the dark hole of the roof.
She watched their shadows lurching
in uneven shafts of artificial light
and tried to understand how anyone
could ever make a space of this.

Downstairs she hunched her back
to step through furniture in wrong rooms,
his engine photographs, his shoes.
She found a table she could lay for tea
when he would come –
squinting through dust, frowning through the plaster
splitting wide above their heads.

Next day she came home to floods of light
knocked in and spread through every room
and where the loft had been
new glass was only just supporting sky
and for the first time she could see
how they had built a frame to hold the emptiness
and air, and she could hardly wait to live in it.

When the builders left he stayed indoors,
closing windows, moving up and down new stairs.
She made tea that stewed and listened
as he cleared his throat, preparing to do something
so important he would never say. Through the news
she heard the drag of mattress as he hauled it
from the spare bed, up into his bright room in the sky.

Today, below him, she is shifting furniture into the garden,
walking with a straight back through her empty rooms.
She lights a bonfire, watches sparks
that burn though smoke and rise past his high window,
waits to sleep without curtains,
spread out like a star in the big bed,
inventing other names for clouds.

Kitchen Beast

It was a mild spring.
No wonder he left the kitchen door ajar,
no wonder the grey-eyed beast came in
and squeezed into the cupboard
underneath the sink.

It was a still and weathered thing
you might mistake for stone, except
in very quiet times, she heard its rasping breath
and, if she sniffed the air,
she thought she could detect a whiff of zoo.

She blamed him, for leaving doors wide open.
He blamed her for showing him
the beast that he'd let in.

It was a case of fear, she knew.
The bulging kitbag packed in minutes,
tow rope, book of knots he grabbed
as he ran for the hills
without a single *sorry* or *goodbye*.

It was a mild night.
She left the kitchen door ajar
and set about creating quite a careful trail
of milky drinks and cabbage leaves and ham,
in little bowls across the floor, for coaxing.

Cut Off

She gathered up our photographs of you
and one by one cut away the high
trees above your head, sliced through
chair legs and discarded all the sky.

You're intact, assembled in a frame
beside her bed. You in thin air.
You somewhere. She can't even name
the town or room you're in. She couldn't care

less but I've spent ages searching the bin
for scraps of garden and the old settee,
to put them back around you, to leave you in
a place you'll know with half a chance to see

the light on in the yard, the kitchen door
still open for you, wider than before.

The Search

Some of them searched the fields.
Strung out like chains
that dragged across the rough land,
they crouched low, never blinking.
One found a plastic bag,
startled a hare that disappeared,
and in less than an hour
they wanted nothing more
than to stretch their backs
and close their eyes at the sky.

Some of them went to the beach
to look for a pile of clothes on the sand,
and they said the tide was so far out
they felt as if they had crossed a shining desert.
They dug up a crab and a magazine,
and under the pebbles they found
more pebbles, the same but wetter
and so more beautiful.

A few of them scoured the hedges,
jabbed with sticks
and plunged their hands in the dark.
They found sheep's wool snagged on thorns,
and a broken plate, and after a while
their fingers were stained
and some were bleeding.

From the river they dredged a cardigan
and on the railway track they found
a snooker cue.

Later they met in a room
with a table and cameras and lights.
They put together everything they had found
and said it was evidence, of you.

And the Map's No Help
(for Gillie in Canada)

Lost in the rain on my own and the map's no help.
I'll sling it in the back and drive
to Ottawa, to East Farndon,
to the house with the drive at the side.
I'll check the mirror for light blue Skodas
and the sky for loons, off-course. You never know,
maybe something's seeping through the sky.

A puddle the size of Hudson Bay on the road.
I'll hold my breath as I drive through.
And you? Are you diving?
Staying under for as long as it takes
to surface clutching something more than mud.

The rhythmic slap and clunk of your canoe
is shifting in this tired engine, in these wiper blades,
and I think I'm on the wrong road in the dark
when a signpost caught in the lights
names somewhere familiar
and somehow, with just one turn of the wheel,
I'm almost there.

The Cardigan

The day before the funeral
they cleared his things away
into boxes, carrier bags, the backs of cars.
She had to be quick off the mark
to save a single trace of him.

She snatched and gathered randomly,
unlikely treasures – a ballpoint pen
repaired with sellotape, a lighter, out of fuel
since he gave up cigarettes again,
an ancient cardigan

shaped by him, its elbows
pouched and thinning,
pockets moulded to his fists
and in them still a crumpled handkerchief,
the wrapper from a Fox's mint.

She laid his cardigan across the bed
and slowly worked her thumbs
around the buttons as she fastened them.
And then she put one finger to her lips

as if to quieten a companion with 'Ssh…',
held it there, then pressed it
to the burn mark from a cigarette,
a stain of paint along one cuff.

She kept it on her bed until they buried him.
And then that night
she locked his pen and lighter in her drawer
and fetched a dustbin bag.

She folded up the cardigan
and placed it carefully inside,
then carried it downstairs
into the darkness of the yard.

This House

I thought that I could only leave this house
if first I could imagine one day coming back
to the empty husk of it,
to someone else's stains on the worn out rug,
their invisible skin.

To be certain I could always picture it,
I walked barefoot in the dark,
until I didn't stub my toe
or miss a turn on the stairs.

But it wasn't enough
so I began to eat this house.

At first I gagged on the thin white walls
and grazed my throat on an edge of light
at the bedroom door,
but soon I could swallow windows whole,
the view of the roof,
the awkward corner above the porch.

Then I was full of it, and no room left
for the silver birch
or the broken chimney under the vine,
or this late October night
when the door opens as if on its own
and this empty house is filled with breathing.

II. ROOM OF LEAVES

Notes for an Autopsy Report: 2.3.94

Female. 70.
Malnutrition: reduction in skin-fold thickness,
lack of adipose tissue, loss of skeletal muscle bulk.
Poor circulation.
Poor nutrition.
Poor hygiene.
Venous ulcers, haematomas, lacerations to both shins,
probably results of minor trauma.
Deep irregular facial lesions. Teeth marks.
PM injury caused by smaller predators.
X-rays show a fractured neck of femur – left.
suggests a fall – shock – hypothermia
likely cause of death.
(See irregular pigmentation, micro infarcts in the brain).

First Romance: 1959

If anyone had asked before today
I could have named the contents
of every single jar of coloured fluid
on the shelves; I could have drawn
the microscopic structure of the liver
and the exact position of the thyroid gland.

I could have labelled them
with just the same precision that it takes
to mix and measure laxatives,
restoratives and preparations
to relieve the common cold.

I had a good eye
and a steady hand.

But today you asked me to the dance
and I accepted
and now I cannot eat or breathe or speak.
I am taking magnesium carbonate in rough doses,
I have developed a shaking palsy
and I have nothing to wear.

Mother will have baked a toad in the hole
and I won't touch it.
She will ask me where I'm going
and I won't say.
She will reprimand me, *Gracie!*
and I will leave the room

to be sick in the lavatory,
to dance with a pillow in my arms,
to just begin to realise
how unhappy I have been.

In Love

Look at me now, mother,
your awkward lump,
dancing with Frank to *Moonglow*
and knowing the words.

I've worn my American stockings to the 3D film
and I'm tipsy on gin.
would you believe it?
Please try

then next time you tell me I stare like a simpleton
perhaps I'll explain how I'm learning
to see Frank's face on the bedroom wall
whenever I choose.

We've been looking at rings, mother.
My favourite is blue.
Please serve a chicken on Sunday
and smile.

Frank's Proposal

I want to start again.
I want to start again
against a New York sky.
Tyrone Power on the thirteenth floor
breathing silk. Will you do it?

I want to board a liner to the USA.
I want to go there.
An Affair to Remember on the open deck,
sky full of stars and Vic Damone.
Remember?

When I become The Man with the Golden Arm
will you save me?
Will you be Kim Novak in a haze of smoke?
Will you help me break the habit of a lifetime?
Will you?

Wedding Dress

If I stand at mother's mirror
I can watch my fingers smooth the stomach
of my half-made dress.
A little stiffness in it hisses
and a tickle runs the length of me.

Sometimes I've made faces in this mirror,
pulled the skin below my eyes
and pushed my shoulders up into my neck
to show thick chins.
I'm no beauty queen. I'm no stripling.

Breathe in, Gracie. No.
Since yesterday I'm breathing out.

I went to Doctor Portlow.
'Don't wait long, you'll need to rest,
but no you're not, you're not too old.'

I watch my lips rehearse the pull
of 'married' 'husband' 'child'.
I'm no desert, mother. I'm no maiden aunt.
I'll be fat with it. I'll be teeming.
I will, Frank. I will.

Egg

I'm opening it early, with mother,
this tiny pink and silver gift
packed in cotton wool. *Take care.*

With hearts entwined, for Grace and Frank,
Your Wedding Day. I move it closer
to the window. *Sit down, girl,*
catch the turquoise, glimpse
a freckled brown beneath the stain of paint.

A blackbird's egg. Stolen
from the nest. An empty shell, so cold.
I'll cradle it. *Don't be absurd.*

I'm stroking it. A crack and then
a shiver runs its length and it's
crazed. *Clumsy ox.* Poor chick.
Poor unborn chick.

Frank in a Fog

I'm in a fog.
I'm in a real pea-souper of a fog.

It started like a mist around my feet,
I've lost my shoes.
I thought I'd gone to heaven but I'd not
and now I'm sinking to my knees
in a fog.

Last night I packed my bag
and carried Joey down to Mrs H
and went to Eddie's with the ring
and counted eight pounds four and nine
in threepenny bits from the savings jar.
I even slept.

But now...

If only I could run once through the words
without a breath.
I must rehearse.
If only I could see to fix my tie
and shut my case
and find the door
and say I love you
but I'm swallowing the fog
and I might just disappear.

Church: November 1960

Grace in the Morris Oxford
fingering ribbons
sick with the smell of petrol
and leatherette seats

and the kindness of Uncle Alfred
patting her arm.
Left up Windsor Avenue
down Harcourt Lane

and back to the church
and Father Broome
is hurrying out to the car
to shake his head.

But Eddie's there
pacing up and down between the graves.
A slow drive. A bitter wind.
I broke an egg today.

Inside the church a whisper
is spreading up the aisle
and Billy leaves
to check with Mrs H

to try The Oak
and the infirmary
and Mrs Langton kneels eyes closed
hands folded on her brow.

Down Marley Crescent
past the shops in Forest Road.
Discount On Soft Furnishings
Tropical Fish For Sale.

Uncle Alfred fidgeting
and looking for words.
We're buying a three-piece suite
on the never-never.

Back onto Windsor Avenue
down Harcourt Lane
and Eileen from the pharmacy
is huddled there inside the porch with Ruth

and Cousin Joyce is wearing
Mr Smedley's winter coat
over her bridesmaid's gown.
What are they waiting for?

Eddie turns away
and cups his hands
and strikes a match
in the freezing air.

Nest

I'm building a nest in the garden
and watching my breath disappear
into splintered trees.
The sky is scratched and freezing;
birds are trapped in it.

I finger veins on damaged leaves
and put my ear to the cracked soil
but there's no pulse.
My nest will be of dead and aching things,
lined with my wedding dress,
decorated with our broken flowers.

I'll sing a marriage song behind my throat
where everything is cold and trapped.
Save me from losing my breath in the hard air.
Save me from screaming like birds
and wondering how things disappear.

I'm setting up home without you,
unpacking my trousseau in a room of leaves,
singing.

Frank on the Edge

If I jumped right now,
if I opened my arms
and fell with a splash
that was louder
than the crack of my head
on the rocks,
would you forgive me?

Or if I told you
that inside my heart
there's a fish
with a two inch hook
in its mouth,
gasping like crazy
and I can't get it out,
would you understand?

See, really I'm a crab
that's wedged itself
so tight in its shell
there's nothing left to do
but light a match under me.

I used to be a jellyfish,
remember?
But I've been clouding over,
drying up.
I need to go back in.
Will you throw me?

Diary

Things to get right next time.

1. Keep out of the house.

For this I have opened the garden umbrellas
and built the nest.

2. Remember to leave the presents wrapped.

For safety I have tied the boxes up
in ribbon and hung them from the trees.
(Pink for a girl and we can watch them when they hatch.)

3. I will be lighter and abstract as air.

I'm rehearsing in fields,
running with the wind to greet you,
almost ready to do the egg dance
with my eyes shut.

Frank Writes a Letter

Dear Grace,
This is Frank, do you remember?
The Man Who Disappeared Without a Trace.
The Man Who Died,
except I didn't and it hurt like heck to be alive.

I don't know if I can ever send this.
I'm feeling like A Man Lost in Space,
far away,
and eleven years too late to even try to say

I'm sorry. Are you married? With a family?
And your mother? Did she cope with the disgrace?
The Vanished Groom.
The Man Without a Chance of ever bringing you the moon.

Grace, do you know that when I left you
I left a piece of my heart I can't replace?
I swear it's true
and if I ever could have married,
if I could have been a man at all,
without a doubt, I would have married you.

P.S. I didn't make it to America.

Waiting To Be Pale as a Star

Someone's mother is in the garden, calling.
Doesn't she know she'll frighten the birds from the trees
and wake every chick?
Doesn't she know that I'm tired of telling her Grace is gone?

Come down from there, come down.
I've bought iced buns.

Ssshh!
I think I'll hide, or sing.
No. I'll be still as a bone.

When it's nearly dark, the bungalow lights up
and I see someone's mother in it, trapped,
pacing up and down and she can hardly breathe.
I know that there's a plate of steaming dinner in the hallway
and the front door always flaps. Hopeless.

Bait. Once you're in you never get back out.
You bang your head on the glass
because you didn't know the glass was there
and if it breaks you die of bleeding
and if it doesn't break you die inside.

Grace, don't do this. Grace was heavy.
Grace wore size 9 shoes,
her fingers damaged everything
and no one wanted

Here is better. Nothing here
to break between you and the sky.
Here you can shiver and know that it keeps you alive.
Here you can wait for as long as it takes
for the tell-tale flutter inside your belly,
the secret scent of hatching,
the day when you can be pale as
you can be smooth as
you can be birds that
Ssshh!
These people only came to help you.
Please Grace. Please.

What They Say

This crazy woman
who will steal umbrellas from your porch,
whose neighbours whisper *hide your babies*,
jilted at the altar, sad,
they say that she was bright,
that she had class.

That's her
in filthy white, face daubed with flour.
Watch her tiptoe over cracks.
Watch her spin and jump at the air.

If you speak
she'll say she's watching how the whiteness turns to grey
before things disappear. *Like milk*, she'll say,
like breath in the sky, like teeth.
She'll say things break more easily than you would ever dream.
She'll show you an egg.

Sometimes she stands quietly in fields
and smooths her stomach with each finger
one by one.
Sometimes she breaks open a sour roar
that splits her throat and empties hedges
and pricks up the ears of dogs that sleep a mile away.

They say she gathers dead leaves for confetti.
They say she has a home.
They say her mother whispered *Grace is grieving*
and hung her head in the street for shame.

Sometimes she smiles.
Sometimes she stands in trees.

Almost Bird

Watch.
I can balance like this for hours,
branched high, with my marble eyes
jabbing at weevils.
And I can crouch with my head cocked
to hear the worms underground.

I'm just waiting for wings now,
for that moment of lift
as the wind takes me.
I'm waiting to hang in the air.

Look, claws.
And here's a lichen
spreading down my broken veins.
Every joint in me is knotted.
Is that good?

I know that I can fill a field
with flapping and I can pitch
the harsh note for alarm.
But I am egg empty. I am cold.
There is a cave in me
and its voice reverberates
along my hollow bones.

Last Hours

I am a pharmacist.
I am Kim Novak.
I am a blackbird
and I have fallen from the sky.

Out in the street
the children are singing
and the priest will remember me,
high as rank sausages,
God rest her soul.

I am a broken hag
with eggs to hatch
and I am emptier now
than I have ever been.

Let me lie beneath these wings
and bring me chicks, Frank.
I am not quite ready to fly.

Frank's Retirement

March feeling like November,
downstairs Mr Metcalf
hangs the rack of morning papers
on the door and coughs in the chill air.

Frank turns the fire up high
and sits beside it
cracking eggshell with the back of his spoon,
picking tea leaves from his tongue.

Soon he'll make a shopping list
and pack stale crusts for the birds.
He'll wave as he passes the back of the shop
but Mr Metcalf will be lost in the news.

Out on the street ladders rasp.
Frank watches for the young painter to climb,
his back held stiff, his knuckles showing white.
Beautiful clouds of breath that fill the sky.

Jilted Woman, 70, Found Dead In Nest Of Leaves.
Through the ceiling Mr Metcalf hears
the strain of some old fifties tune.
He taps his foot as he reads

and Frank glides in a perfect arc
across the room,
drowning in silk,
embracing the perfumed air.

The Discovery

PC Ainsley said this was the strangest trail
he'd ever followed; Boffin thought it was surreal,
the supermarket eggs in clusters in the grass,
empty boxes hanging from the trees, pink ribbon
everywhere.

There was almost a path through the bushes and weeds and
      the garden was small
but they took their time and found her old umbrella first
discarded nearby, one rusted spoke bent out,
black nylon jutting like the broken wing of a bird.
Then *What the fuck?*

as Boffin saw the canopy of bright umbrellas.
He waited for Ainsley to pass him and tried not to breathe through
      his nose.
He didn't want the stench, the state of her half-eaten face,
the makeshift bed of twigs and rotting cloth. He turned
and was sick in the grass.

Ainsley crouched low to look at her, the skirt caught up
around her knees, the bare legs thick with grime and tangled
veins. And her face. A strand of matted hair had strayed
across her open mouth and he wanted to smooth it away;
he wanted to tidy her.

Later they noticed the broken tree and Ainsley remembered
nesting when he was a lad, how he fell one day, how he cradled
the eggs in his jumper and carried them home to shoeboxes packed
with cotton wool and labelled: cuckoo, song thrush, sparrow,
blackbird, wren.

Half a battered suitcase in the undergrowth,
a screwtop jar with nothing in it but a ring,
a tarnished ring, set with a clear blue stone.
Ainsley held it to the light. *Poor bitch.*

III. TRUE STORIES

The Bone Beneath The Skin
(after Paula Rego)

The Little Murderess

She has carried the painted chair
from her room at the top of the house
to the edge of this open place
to remember there once was a time
when she wasn't too big for it.
Now she could topple it over
the gaudy rim of the world
with the tip of her tongue.

See this wooden ox and cart
she's loved ever since she crawled
over every floor with it.
Who has so carefully hammered
eight bright spikes in its back?

Things change. Things stay the same.

This dark green dress she will keep forever,
buttoned up to the clean white neck in it,
feeling her stifled muscle leap at the hem of her sleeve,
the bodice strain across her hard flat chest.

Did she slip the sash from round her waist
to play at blind man's buff with it,
or pull the ox and cart
or hear the snap in the air
as she tugged it hard and suddenly
between her fat squeezed hands?

No.
See how she stares beyond the empty grey-white gown,
her certain eyes, the bone beneath the skin.
She has plaited fresh mistletoe into her hair
and, even now, the stain of red is in her shadow.
She is intent on this.

Fixed in a world that is full of her,
leaning into the thrill of what comes next.

The Policeman's Daughter

The moon's a searchlight on the window,
I'm a princess in a tower, with only
blue and shadows out there on the empty street.
Besides, the drop's too far.

I'll pace the room instead,
I'll sit astride your leather chair
and press my thumbs into the tight gold studs
until they dent my skin.

I'll polish boots for you.

Push my hand in deep and wedge my fist
into your cold, ungiving heel, spit,
and feel the rub and drag
of dampened cloth on hide.

I'll sigh and rock
into the rhythmic squeak
until my knuckles blister
and my wrist aches and my fingers burn,

then suddenly I'll feel the rush of sliding
over ice, effortless and smooth,
to make a mirror of your jutting foot,
to find my face at last, in its cold black glare.

Red Monkey

Hunched over his easel with his face set hard,
Red Monkey's painting pictures of himself.
His palette's dull.
He's daubing only red on red on red.

So, did you beat your wife, Red Monkey?
Did she take the scissors to your tail
with one clean snip that severed muscle,
made you vomit on the parquet floor?

And did you see The Lion next day?
Was that his cock or just a giant umbrella in his hands?
Was he offering her a good time
or a temporary kind of shelter from the storm?

She liked his width and length you know,
she even liked his ragged mane
but Dog was standing by, so green and sad,
and what were you doing there?

No wonder she went yellow, sprouted wings,
turned into Butterfly. *One day to live,
a crazy kind of suicide*, you said, Red Monkey,
Lion, Dog, *One day to live.*

Try this: one day to fly,
one day to dance, alone and high and free
in the cool white air.
Paint that, Red Monkey, if you dare.

Torch Song

She stuffed it in her briefcase not to scare the crowds
and carried it for miles,
on trains, through car parks, down the rush hour streets.
It glowed a little, scorched her papers,
melted down her sandwiches, and made the world
inedible, illegible, a dangerous place.

Outside his door at last she hesitated, knew
she mustn't start a blaze
in there, was terrified of what one wisp
of smoke could signal to the air.
She left it on the pavement, went inside, and watched
as people gathered on the street all afternoon,

to warm their hands on it, to stare: a burning torch
inside a briefcase, smoking,
flaming now despite the steady rain
that specked the window so he noticed
hardly anything until the crowd began
to sing – a little out of key at first, unsteady

in the rhythm, then a harmony, a chorus,
building clear and almost
beautiful, that had him on his feet
and running, nearly through the door
before she reached him, pulled him back, pushed past, and all
without a thought that for a second she had held him.

In a heat haze, eyes that stung until they soaked
her face, she grabbed the briefcase,
burnt her fingers, clung on tight, and ran,
down back streets, alleys, over walls.
It lit her route the whole way home, kept men at bay,
until she reached her door and sat awake all night,

watched her torch as it burned brightly in the yard,
as he lay miles away,
unsettled, half remembering strangers singing,
dreamt a spark ignited curtains,
flared across his room and burst into a wall
of flame, to burn him down, to burn his whole world down.

True Story
(for Alan Southgate)

When he came in that night
the cat was yowling, he says, and pacing the house
and her kittens, just four days old,
had gone from the box.

He followed her into the kitchen
and watched her scratch at the cupboard door
and he says that her fur was standing on end
and her tail was swollen with fright

and when he opened the door
she made a noise that caught in her throat
and she edged away
and there, at the back of the shelf,

behind the jars and the cans of soup,
was the darker shape of a tiny tabby cat.

He says that he reached in and felt it warm and soft,
with such relief he didn't wonder anything
until the dampness reached his fingers
as he eased it out and he saw

the head lolled back and that its throat
was slit across and it was dead.
and he says he felt a twist in his gut
and his legs were shaking hard

as he fetched a hammer and paced the house
with the cat, like a madman, calling,
lifting cushions, peering into the dark
and then, behind the bathroom door,

he found the second kitten
lying in the blood drained from its open neck.

He was frantic, he says, he was terrified,
moaning as loud as the cat
as he turned away, as she scratched
at the bedroom door, as he opened it,

followed her in, and almost straight away
and maybe worst of all,
found the ginger kitten, the last born,
in the cupboard drawer beside his bed.

All of them warm, all of them dead,
all with a slit in the throat.

He says he went back to the kitchen
and counted the knives,
that he checked every window and door,
and examined the cat for signs of a fight.

That night he left every light on
and slept on the couch
with the cat on his legs
and a knife in his hand

and he says that he was still
clutching it tight
when the morning eventually came and he says
that this story is true.

The Gifts

You told me that I'd landed on your doorstep
like a totally inexplicable delivery
of laminated knitting patterns,
handed you a piping hot tripe supper
and a Co-op bag of dog-eared Mills & Boons.

You said it didn't help to know
that these were gifts of love.

And ever since you've looked at me
as though I'm bearing half a sack
of build-your-own-authentic-light-up Taj Mahal kits
just for you, and always dress to meet me
in your weather-beater balaclava, cover-all protector suit
and cockroach pumps.

I'd like to talk.
I'd really like to say a word or two.

But last night when I called on you
my footsteps activated garden gnomes
with powerful beams inside their hats,
your doorbell triggered angry guard-dog sound effects,
so I went home

and sat among the old, familiar clutter
in my living room – the electric whirlpool foot spa,
Jeffrey Archer hardbacks, karaoke tape
of *Wartime Love Songs Volume 2* –
every one of them a gift from you.

Lost Property

Racks of lost coats pushed together,
dreaming arms in their arms,
fingers buttoning, unbuttoning,
a warmth inside,

and boxes of umbrellas, upright, closed,
their nylon whispering at the rain
against the window, bent spokes straining
in a kind of reaching out.

A single leather gauntlet, still half-shaped
around the grip of handlebar,
still holding on, the roar and rush of air
against its back.

At his desk the clerk records the details
of discovery, attaches labels
to a broken doll, a brand new pair of shoes,
another coat, a hat.

He's sick of it, the stale smell of forgotten things,
the aftertaste of loss.
Beneath his desk he keeps old magazines:
Mayfair, Penthouse,

Annie, 23, from Stockholm
stares at him. He knows she's aching for it,
runs his finger down her body,
makes her wait.

Strong Hands

I say I'm a good man,
good as any man.
Winter, summer, I can tell the time by the light,
walk the road for fourteen hours.
See. Strong hands.
I stink like an old dog fox
but I'm good as any man.

I gave the girl a roof above her head
and she stole milk from me.
I cleared the dog dirt down at the track
and the boys sent me into the hedge
for a box of food.
Tricking bastard. Shits.
A nest full of wasps and I'd seventy stings.
No wonder I dream.

I can show you the scar
where they had my stomach out when Irene went,
the bitch. I'd hang her from that branch
with my bare hands. No.
Dig a pit. Kick her down.

I'd not do that to a dog. Or a cat.
I'd not do that to a fly.
I'm a good man.

I ran with the fox, old devil.
Did you see that?
Over the gardens, along at the back.

They said in the Kwik Save
I stink like an old dog fox.
You're barred. You're barred.
You're not the fucking Queen, I said,
you're a shit, and the day they cut off the gas
I wiped my arse on their letter
and sent it back.

I'm just as good a man.

I'll do your garden,
do your garden for you now.
See. Strong hands.

The Man Who's Afraid

The man who's afraid of artificial light
finds winter hard.
He uses daylight hours to steal
the dynamos from children's bikes,
to check for streetlamps in the lane
and dig his garden deep enough
to bury broken bulbs.

And he eats. He has to eat.
Veg from the allotment, tins and fruit
from Dawkins Corner Grocery
on brave and sunny days.
His fridge is dark.

Along the mantelpiece he keeps
a radio that's stuck with plasters
to conceal the glow, a dictionary
scored with thick black lines through
ultraviolet, sodium, main beam.

He sleeps badly,
dreams of living on a flight path,
has to keep a gun beneath his pillow
just in case someone is lost
and drives a car
up the track to his house
before first light.

Chin

At first it wasn't so bad.
Plenty of stroking and tickling,
soothing creams and treated like I mattered.
But then, the day before his fourteenth birthday,
I came out in spots. Revolting.
Felt so ill I could have died.
And what did he do?
Scrubbed me with something that stank,
just about set me on fire.
He had me weeping, bleeding,
angrier than I knew I could be,
and, worst of all, his friends would point
and laugh while he just sat there,
pressing me into the heel of his hand,
planning the day he'd be old enough
to cover me up for good.
I hardly moved. I itched, burned,
knew I was scarred for life,
doubted the world could get much harder.
Wrong.
Imagine, you wake one morning to find
a spike's grown out of your guts in the night.
And the next week another, another.
You're faint all the time, afraid
to catch sight of yourself in the mirror,
to see how you've changed, for the worse.
In the end I was glad when I vanished, went under
and stayed there. It's hard, but I'm learning
a new way of breathing. I'm learning to see in the dark.

Remembering Jesus

The man on the moped had sewn a badge
to his fluorescent orange coat,
Jesus Is With Me.
From his handlebars a purple pennant waved,
Don't Forget The Lord,
but he was quite alone.

Shoppers called to him,
'Excuse me, you've forgotten...'
but he'd indicated left and gone,
unsteady as he cornered,
surely noticing no hands around his waist,
a lack of weight at the back.

Imagine the awful moment when he realised.
Tears steaming his visor, the cries of despair.
How he must have backtracked
every inch of his journey,
grabbing at bearded strangers, searching for signs –
a sandal with a broken strap,
white sheet in a ditch.

People say he left his job that day
to make a life of door-to-door enquiries,
fixing posters onto empty walls.
Seek and Ye Shall Find.
He accelerates along the high street.
I Shall Follow Jesus All My Days.

On the Phone

No, she's not afraid of the stairs.
She's afraid to stand at the top of the stairs
and sometimes also to look up the stairs
but she's not afraid of the stairs.

Yes, she dreams she floats down the stairs.
She's dressed but her feet are bare;
the streetlight is blue and then black.
No, she's not afraid to float down the stairs,

but, yes, to land at the foot of the stairs
and to have to go on, or walk back up the stairs,
either feels bad, she says something's there.
No, it's invisible – and near the stairs.

She doesn't let anyone else on the stairs
except, she says, animals live on the stairs
in the daylight, but not when it's dark.
No, she's not scared of them – they guard the stairs.

The wallpaper's scratched at the top of the stairs
and ripped at the bottom – and stained.
No, she's not damaged the stairs,
she's not afraid of the stairs.

Fisherman's Tale

Do you know the puzzle of the smallest man in the world
found hanged in his caravan, only clues a walking stick
and a pile of shavings under the bed?
Well, I'm his brother. I know how he died
and it wasn't anything like the way they said.

Some of it's here in my little book of photos.
That's him in the grand ring just the week before.
That's our dear old mam at his side.
She adored him. Finished her off
when they made a game of guessing how he died.

Here's Reggie White whose wife was crushed to death
by a falling pig in Leeds in 1983.
I knew him. He was a decent bloke.
Always reckoned he could have handled the grief
but he couldn't live with a death turned into a joke.

These next three pages are some of the biggest fish
that Mr Holdaway caught and that's his sister, June,
the poor girl who was so distressed.
There's a shot of the phone box where he died
with the phone off the hook and a ten-inch carp on his chest.

I was the one he'd been talking to at the time,
the first to arrive at the tragic scene, the nearest thing
to a witness, DC Rainbow said.
In the end I got sick of his questions, sick of the smirk
in his eyes that I call a lack of respect for the dead.

Of course I knew Mr Holdaway, he caught the carp.
At least ten inches, yes, two panes were smashed. Outside.
I wanted to save him and knew I would fail.
His hands were covered in blood. This isn't a game
This isn't some kind of a blasted fisherman's tale.

Amnesiac

Walking into half a room where sky has fallen in.
The stench of old men's piss and startling blue
where walls, mirror, dressing table
should have been.

The dream of an ear – eye in a black canal
that echoes wind; the tubes, the cavern,
then a kind of twisted spilling into space.
This place.

A bench by a river, any river,
clothes that could be any man's: grey suit,
waist 34, chest 38, grey socks, white underwear.
I'm anywhere.

Practise: *Doctor, Officer, I don't know who I am.*
There's something brown beneath my nails.
It could be soil, it could be Worcester sauce, it could be blood.
I haven't dared to smell it, haven't dared to suck and see.

A film where someone's sinking in the sand,
his fingers inches from a tree, or hanging
by his nails a hundred storeys up.
He's slipping, letting go, not quite connecting. Me.

I've checked my pockets twenty seven times.
I haven't found a photograph or wallet or a key.
Eleven five pound notes and four pound thirty-eight.
It's late.

I'm walking into half a room where sky has fallen in.
The stench of old men's piss and startling blue
where walls, mirror, dressing table
should have been

How to Disappear

First rehearse the easy things.
Lose your words in a high wind,
walk in the dark on an unlit road,
observe how other people mislay keys,
their diaries, new umbrellas.
See what it takes to go unnoticed
in a crowded room. Tell lies:
I love you. I'll be back in half an hour.
I'm fine.

Then childish things.
Stand very still behind a tree,
become a cowboy, say you've died,
climb into wardrobes, breathe on a mirror
until there's no one there, and practise magic,
tricks with smoke and fire –
a flick of the wrist and the victim's lost
his watch, his wife, his ten pound note. Perfect it.
Hold your breath a little longer every time.

The hardest things.
Eat less, much less, and take a vow of silence.
Learn the point of vanishing, the moment
embers turn to ash, the sun falls down,
the sudden white-out comes.
And when it comes again – it will –
just walk at it, walk into it, and walk,
until you know that you're no longer
anywhere.